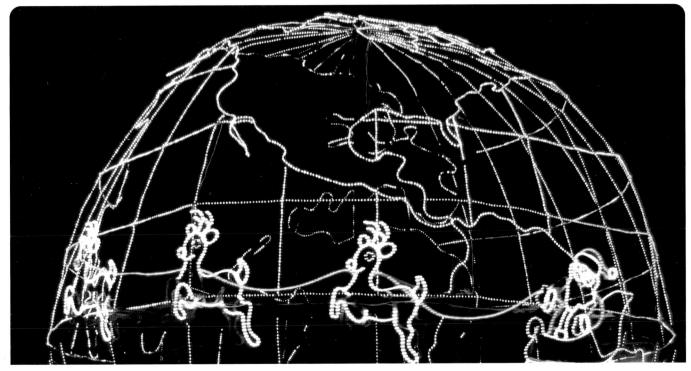

Planet Christmas

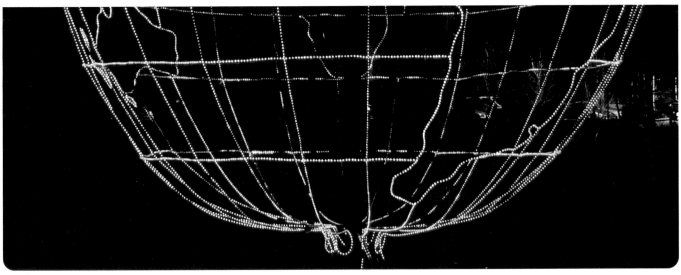

First published in
Great Britain in 2005 by
Collins & Brown
The Chrysalis Building
Bramley Road
London W10 6SP

An imprint of Chrysalis Books Group plc

1 3 5 7 9 8 6 4 2

British Library Cataloguing-in-Publication Data: A catalogue
record for this book is available from the British Library.

ISBN 1 84340 325 0

Commissioning by Chris Stone
Packaged by Justyn Barnes and Aubrey Ganguly at Aubergine
Designed by Paul Sinclair at Parallax Studios

Thanks to Matt Phillips

Reproduction by Anorax Ltd
Printed and bound by Imago, Singapore

Front cover photo: DPA Deutsche-Press-Agentur/ DPA/Empics
Back cover photos: Duncan Ballentine, Marcel Labrosse

Every effort has been made to credit the photos in this book
correctly. Please contact Chrysalis Books if you identify any
errors and we will correct in future editions.

2

Planet Christmas

The world's most extreme Christmas decorations!

Chuck Smith

COLLINS & BROWN

foreword
by Chuck Smith

Every community has that one house decorated more extravagantly for Christmas than any other in the area. That house is the one people like me want to out-do when we decorate our own. It doesn't take long to figure out it's much easier said than done.

If you're lucky enough to live in the most distinctive house, you earn year-round bragging rights as "the Christmas guy". In the beginning you don't realize it, but soon you discover that coming over to see your house has become a holiday season tradition for many families. Once you understand how you are affecting others and the life-long memories you are creating, you get bitten by a bug with no known cure – you're a Christmas decorating enthusiast and you're not alone.

In this book you will see pictures from around the world of homes with truly over-the-top displays (plus some of the most spectacular public shows), and read the testimonies of the people who created them. These are the folk who think about their decorations all year long and how they can top their previous efforts. Many make huge investments in their displays, accepting massive electrical bills as an inevitable consequence of their efforts to brighten up the neighborhood. Other homes are decorated more modestly, but still look beautiful during the holiday season.

As you will discover, these decorating enthusiasts have different reasons for going to such extreme lengths, but they all seem to share a common motivation – this is their way of making a real difference in the community by sharing the joy of Christmas with everyone.

It doesn't matter if you live in a tiny flat or on a huge plantation, decorating for the season is fun and creates lasting family traditions. As you look through this book, appreciate Planet Christmas. I hope you enjoy this festive visual feast and get some great ideas on how you can make your home special and finally outshine your neighbor down the road!

Chuck Smith - Founder, PlanetChristmas.
www.planetchristmas.com

Santa & the Teddies!

"WE DELIGHTED VISITORS WITH ARTIFICIAL SNOW WHICH WE PUMPED OUT FROM OUR BALCONY."

"We light up every year and try to make the presentation different and interesting so that it appeals to both young and old and brings the Christmas spirit back into their lives. We had over 35,000 visitors in 2004, causing traffic jams backing up some distance from our street.

"In 2004, the display was made up not only of lights, but also two stages which we built in the garage and guestroom (both face the street and driveway). In one, we had a lit-up nativity scene, and in the other, the 'Santa And The Teddies' band, complete with instruments and disco lights, all behind a perspex frontage.

"We supported the SPCA (the Royal New Zealand Society for Prevention of Cruelty to Animals) and had their donation box in front of the teddy bear display which proved to be most rewarding.

"Furthermore, we delighted visitors with artificial snow which we pumped out from our balcony. With the chill that winter in New Zealand we were not far from reality on some nights as the flakes settled on the driveway."

Duncan, Margie, Charles and Tracey Ballentine
North Shore City, Auckland, New Zealand

'Santa And The Teddies', playing gigs nightly in the Ballentine family's garage, proved to be a great attraction!

They've got plenty of inflatables too...

Artificial snow is pumped out from the balcony.

Around 35,000 visitors came to see the Ballentine's incredible 2004 display in North Shore City, New Zealand.

Duncan, Charles, Margie and Tracey Ballentine stand proudly in front of their amazing display.

Santa says, "Hi!"

Drive-by photo shoot!

"**M**y husband Tom took these pictures driving home from church the day after Christmas, using the camera he'd given me as a present. This house is well known in this area for its extreme display.

"It reminds me of my childhood in Clairton, Pennsylvania. There was a family whose house looked sort of like a gingerbread house, with Santa and nine reindeer on the roof. I have a vivid memory of standing at the local grocery store and seeing that house from a distance, all lit up... on Valentine's Day!"

Tiffany Baxendell
Peters Township, Pennysylvania, USA

Brightening up Seaford

"ONE OF OUR NEIGHBOUR'S CHILDREN CAME BACK FROM HOSPITAL AFTER HAVING A CANCEROUS TUMOUR REMOVED. HE SAW THE LIGHTS AND HIS EYES LIT UP. IT GAVE HIM A REAL BOOST."

"We originally started out doing the lights to celebrate the year 2000, with just a simple '2000' written on the wall in fairy lights. Since then we have expanded each year. For 2004, we used about 5,000 lights and created a simple countdown timer showing how many days left until Christmas.

"There is no real reason for us decorating the house, apart from to try and liven up the neighbourhood, as we are the only ones in the street to decorate our house. Most of my friends think it's a bit odd that I put in so much hard work for something you can't even see when you're indoors. But as we live quite near a school for 4-11 year old children, a lot of kids and parents take a detour during December to walk past and look at the lights.

"The most memorable moment was when one of our neighbour's children came back from hospital after having a cancerous tumour removed and as he came round the corner of the street and saw the lights, his eyes lit up. It gave him a real boost after being in hospital for about a month. This then made his mum cry as it was the first time she'd seen him happy in months."

Craig and Michael Woolgar
Seaford, East Sussex, England

The talking
Snowpeople

"What makes our Christmas display so unique is that I made my wife, Konnie, two real snowpeople. They are called Marie and Boudreaux and they never melt because there is six tons of refrigeration running to keep them frozen! They are both five-feet tall, have eyes made of coal and carrot noses. He has a Santa hat, she has a Christmas apron and a bonnet, and between seven and nine 'o' clock each evening, they talk to the children!

"We have won and placed in the neighborhood Christmas display contest for the last three years. Our next-door neighbor, Dale, tries to keep up a kinda contest between us, but he just can't."

Steve and Konnie Higginbottom
Kenner, Louisiana, USA

Swedish style

"WHEN WE TAKE THE LIGHTS DOWN, WE STORE THE MAIN BULBS IN A BIG, OLD TRUNK THAT WAS MADE IN THE 1880s."

We lived in America for two years and we really liked the Christmas decorations there so we brought the tradition with us when we moved back to Sweden a few years ago.

"We have a reindeer on the balcony, a Santa on the garage wall and around 4,500 bulbs - mainly curtains, bows and garlands in lots of different colours. The bulbs around the balcony flash. When we take the lights down, we store the main bulbs in a big, old trunk that was made in the 1880s (pictured) and the larger decorations are stored in the attic.

"Compared to some American displays, ours is small, but it is not that common for Swedish people to decorate their houses. In our area there are only a couple of houses (including ours) that have more decorations than the usual outdoor Christmas tree and the electrical advent candlestick in the windows. People stop their cars and take pictures of our house. Even some tourist buses are passing the house at a slow speed.

"We want to buy more decorations in US where they are cheaper and there's more choice. But it's difficult to bring them back because they don't always fit in a suitcase!

Pia and Torbjorn Lindbeck
Ljungsbro, Sweden

Holiday train

"This train was decorated with 8,000 Christmas lights in December 2001 as it travelled from Montreal to Vancouver to encourage donations to food banks in Canada and the USA."

Lights on the move

"Headlights working... check. Brake lights... double check. Christmas lights... triple check!"

crimbo caravan

"An old caravan gets a festive makeover."

23

From the heart

"THE EMPLOYEES AT WAL-MART WILL GET IN NEW MERCHANDISE AND CALL ME AT HOME TELLING ME THEY HAVE PUT SOME STUFF ASIDE FOR ME TO LOOK AT."

"We started our light display in 1996 with three single strands of curtain lights. Of course, the display grew to 40,000 lights after that (we also decorate for Halloween with around 25,000 lights).

"Our house is a focal point at both Halloween and Christmas. We draw over 1,000 trick-or-treaters and have a multitude of cars for the Christmas Holiday. Luckily, our neighbors enjoy the display and look forward to the first of November each year as my son and I bring out the Christmas lights. Even the employees at Wal-Mart will get in new merchandise and call me at home telling me they have put some stuff aside for me to look at.

"We have many beautiful homes in our area and unfortunately these homes are rarely decorated. My wife says its because people are not as 'fanatical' as my son and I. Also, the $500 light bill in January may be a deterrent to some... ouch! But you have to do this from the heart and for no other reason..."

Michael Wright
Fayetteville, Tennessee, USA

Down by the waterfront

"A horse-drawn carriage trots in front of this sharply-lit house in Springfield, Massachusetts, USA."

Two to make a dream come true

"These are two houses in South Avenue, Lyme Regis, must just have been the most decorated in Britain in 2004. There were traffic jams as everyone slowed down to have a look."

Marcel's magical display

**"A CITY BUS STOPPED IN FRONT OF MY HOUSE...
THE DRIVER WANTED TO THANK ME AND SAY THAT MY
DISPLAY MAKES HIM SMILE WHILE HE'S DOING HIS JOB."**

"I started doing this for the kids of the area. They really love to see a house decorated up with lots of lights. Now, I think I do it because I really love to sit at my window, or outside and watch how the house I've decorated makes other people so happy. In 2004, a city bus stopped in front of my house while I was putting the final touches to the display. The bus had passengers in it, but the driver stopped anyway. He just wanted to thank me and say that my display makes him smile while he is doing his job. That means a lot to me.

"I love the entire display but if I had to pick just one thing, it would have to be the Santa and reindeer on the side of the house. It is unique and our house is set up perfectly to display it. You can see the side of our house for almost two blocks totally unobstructed. The children just love to see that particular animation every year.

"We usually tell everyone in the family when the lights are going on and they show up that night for a lighting ceremony. We all stand outside and at the push of a button, the lights are officially started for the season. It just wouldn't be Christmas without it now. It's become a part of our holidays, like trimming the tree.

Marcel Labrosse
Stoney Creek, Ontario, Canada

Brad and his 400 blowmolds!

"**I**t takes me a month to put my display up – I start as soon as my Halloween stuff comes down. I do it all on my own – the only help I get is someone to hold the buggy during the after-Christmas sales rush!

"My favorite decorative feature is the blowmolds (light-up plastic Santas etc...). I have 400 and some are twice my age or older. They can be very hard to find and are fun to collect. They take up a lot of storage but are worth it as most people do not use them anymore.

"Right now I have two 10'x9' sheds full of decorations, lights, inflatables, and so on. I also have a 100-year-old barn that I store all the blowmolds in. It's almost full now.

"I do it as a way to spread the Christmas cheer to all the kids and adults alike, but also to tell others about my religion.

"My dad thinks I am crazy. My friends used to compete with me until it got so large and now they think I am crazy too. My girlfriend loves it, though, and hopefully I will have her to help me out and support my hobby.

"When we have party guests they love it and talk about it. They keep looking out for planes trying to land in the yard!"

Brad Caudill
Chapin, South Carolina, USA

Skyscraper trees!

"This 33-metre-tall tree (with 33,000 lights) in Sydney for Christmas 2000 was claimed to be the largest in the southern hemisphere."

"This amazing 174-feet-tall tree was built in Ibirapuera Park in Sao Paulo, Brazil to celebrate Christmas 2004."

Happy holidays
from the Griswal... er. Bixlers!

**"MY FRIENDS THINK I'VE LOST MY MIND, BUT
I DO IT FOR THE LOVE OF CHRISTMAS, THE
LOVE OF LIGHTS... AND FOR FUN."**

"Our light display goes all the way around the house, including the backyard and my daughter's playhouse. It makes my daughter the hit of her class in school!

"We started out with about 5,000 lights in 1991, but every year we add something new. Our 2004 display consisted of over 50,000 lights as well as inflatables, silhouettes, plastic forms, plus an FM Broadcaster we introduced the year before.

"My friends think I've lost my mind, but I do it for the love of Christmas, the love of lights... and for fun.

"A couple of years after we began doing this regularly, we were in a mobile home park. I was setting up the display and a couple of the neighbors began calling me Clark (as in the Griswalds) so I decided to put up a sign in the front yard 'Happy Holidays from The Griswalds.' This sign has been part of our display for over 10 years and when I put the sign in the ground, it signals that the display is complete."

Don Bixler
Holland, Ohio, USA

42,500

Hi, my name is Todd Smith. My display consists of:

- ✳ 42,500 shining Christmas lights
- ✳ 365 days of planning
- ✳ 150 amps of electrical power
- ✳ 60 hours of set-up
- ✳ 10 hard-working Smith family members
- ✳ 9 playful reindeer
- ✳ 8 dancing Christmas trees
- ✳ 7 computer controllers
- ✳ 6 majestic angels
- ✳ 5 woolly sheep
- ✳ 4 busy elves
- ✳ 3 wise men
- ✳ 2 jolly Santa Clauses
- ✳ 1 peaceful manger

Todd Smith
Temecula, California

Beat the neighbor!

"THE BIGGEST REASON THIS ALL STARTED WAS A BET I MADE WITH MY NEIGHBOR, TIM."

"I'm actually surprised that some of the neighbors haven't complained. On most weekend nights, the street is blocked by traffic at times. Tour buses are now frequent and between 10,000 and 20,000 visitors came by last year.

"Perhaps the biggest reason that this all started, was a bet I made with my neighbor, Tim, down the road. He always does a big Halloween display and he used to blow me out of the water. In 2002, though, he was impressed with my lights, so in the spring of 2003 we challenged each other to a Christmas light display contest. Tim was talking robotics, tens of thousands of lights etc. By mid-November, I had invested lots of money and effort into my display, but Tim still hadn't began to set up. I thought that maybe he'd begin next weekend. It wasn't until the week before light-up night that he told me, 'I can't afford it this year, you're on your own... you win'. Needless to say, he can never catch me now!

"For 2005, I am computerizing the display. We are also going to start fund-raising this year for the Cancer Society, but, to be honest, that is not a reason for doing it, just a fringe benefit."

Dan Lagerstrom
Surrey, British Columbia, Canada

Net of lights

"Known as 'Christmas House', Ehrhard and Christiane Osmer of Bremen Habenhausen have wrapped their home in a net of lights."

Holiday in the hills

"I HAVE FOUR MOVING REINDEERS, A ROCKING HORSE AND AN ICE-SKATING SNOWMAN."

"My family and friends thought I was crazy when I started seven years ago, but now they think it's cool. My wife gets into the spirit and always helps me with buying the additional decorations. My daughter thinks it is great – she always invites her friends over to hang out while they are on.

"I put up around 12,000 lights. Most of them are miniature lights. I use both still, motion and blinking lights to show action and I like animation so I have four moving reindeers, a rocking horse and an ice-skating snowman.

"I always put up my display during the Thanksgiving holidays, but I have to do a lot of prep work weeks ahead. I have to pull everything down from the rafters in my garage and then check that everything is in working order. Then I sit out front and stare at my home plotting how I am going to set things up.

"It's tricky to connect everything without tripping the breakers or blow fuses in the strings. The second problem is staking and securing the displays to withstand the Santa Ana winds that I get here in Anaheim Hills. They can gust up to 70 miles per hour when they hit which isn't conducive to Christmas decorations!"

Michael Girard
Anaheim, California, USA

Candy Cane
House

"THIS YEAR I ADDED A 16-FOOT-TALL HELICOPTER ON THE TOP OF MY ROOF WITH A STROBE RUDDER FOR AN AWESOME EFFECT"

"My family and I started going a little crazy about seven years ago. The theme of the house is, of course, candy cane and as it took on a life of its own it became known as the 'Antioch Candy Cane House'. We enjoy a growing following of people each year as they wait to see what else we have added to our display.

"Our 35-foot, 2,400-light, home-made candy cane, is a real show-stopper. Along with the front-yard grass, which is completely covered in green lights, it is powered by an eight-channel strobe controller which make the cane and the lawn dance all night to various patterns.

"In my latest display, I added a 16'x8' helicopter on the top of my roof with a strobe rudder for an awesome effect."

Frank & Mary Rehm
Antioch, California, USA

Bright Eye

"A Christmas light show at the stunning London Eye a.k.a the Millennium Wheel."

Firefighter
sets his house alight!

"MY FAVORITE THING IS THE LIGHTED TRAIN DISPLAY. IT WAS GIVEN TO ME BY MY SON FOR CHRISTMAS..."

" I start the first of November and it takes most of the month when I'm not working at my job (I'm a firefighter/paramedic) to set up. The goal is to light the display by 1 December or the weekend after Thanksgiving. I usually work on the display from four to six hours per day and average about ten to 14 days to put up the display. Usually I do almost all of the work by myself, but my wife, Wendy, is the artistic director and she tells me where to place the displays in the yard from across the street.

"My favorite thing is the lighted train display. It was given to me by my son for Christmas several years ago. I have always liked trains and enjoy looking at it. Previously, I had a smaller train that didn't really show up but now this is a centerpiece of the yard display."

Jon Fiedler
Ellicot City, Maryland, USA

The neatest display in Woodway

"**W**e have won the Woodway Christmas Decorating contest the last three years in a row. We have hand-built many of the decorations in our yard and all of our lighted animated displays were made by me and my dad, Ed. Dad helps me a great deal and so do my two brothers, Kyle and Mike, and my mom, Billie. My nephew Dylan also gives us a hand. It takes about 10 days working an average of five to six hours a day.

"We do it because we love Christmas and we love to see the faces of kids in the cars driving by looking at it. We have friends that drive over 90 miles just to come see it every Christmas. Everybody loves it and offers to help.

"We get told by so many people that it's the neatest display they have ever seen. That makes it all worthwhile."

Dustin Chapman
Woodway, Texas, USA

51

Pensacola Lights

"IT HAS TURNED INTO A YEAR-ROUND HOBBY INCORPORATING ALL OF MY VARIED INTERESTS IN ART, MUSIC, ELECTRONICS, COMPUTERS, ENGINEERING, DESIGN, CARPENTRY AND ELECTRICAL WIRING…"

"'Pensacola Lights' began a few years ago when my wife and I decided to invite our entire family to Thanksgiving Day dinner at our house. We had over 30 guests that year, so we decided to go all out and put up 5,000 Christmas lights to get everyone in the holiday spirit. Our family really enjoyed the display, so I immediately started to plan how to make it even more exciting for the following Thanksgiving Day gathering.

"Since then, 'Pensacola Lights' has continued to grow and evolve into a display featuring over 50,000 lights. It has turned into a year-round hobby incorporating all of my varied interests in art, music, electronics, computers, engineering, design, carpentry and electrical wiring. I love Christmas music and the ability to synchronize the lights to the music is what sets 'Pensacola Lights' apart from any other display in the area.

"'Pensacola Lights' is our holiday gift to our community. We believe in doing things together as a family and establishing holiday traditions that will be remembered by our children.

"In September 2004, we were devastated by Hurricane Ivan and many people thanked me for my efforts in brightening up the neighborhood.

Dennis K. Johnson
Pensacola, Florida, USA

I'm lovin' it!

"I have been decorating for about 15 years and it has grown from about 500 lights to close on 70,000. It takes a week to get everything up. My lifelong best friend Paul Wood and his eldest sons Phillip and Allen all help to set up.

"I do it because I love it, and I love the season, and I love to see and hear the children when they come by. They all love it and only a few of them think I am crazy."

Darren Shell
Salisbury, North Carolina, USA

Lillian's lights

"This house, pictured in 2001 is owned by grandmother of ten, Lillian Bostock and her husband Derick. Their collection of Santas, reindeer and strings of fairy lights had cost the couple thousands over the years, but she felt the money was well spent, just to see the look of delight on children's faces."

Owen Humphreys
Cowgate, Newcastle, England

Blown away

"Blow-up figures are becoming more and more popular, but I have never seen such a display with so many in one small yard. I just happened to drive by the house and thought I would snap a few pictures of it."

Josh D
Auburn, New York, USA

At home with an
Osborn!

"WHEN PEOPLE LOVE AND APPRECIATE WHAT I'VE DONE… WELL, THAT'S IT FOR ME!"

"My 2004 Display consisted of 46,000 lights (minis and rope light), 52 curtain strobes and utilized 144 channels of Light-O-Rama (LOR) computer-controlled boards. Lights were synchronized to music on six different songs/programs. Music is played through a special transmitter so my neighbors don't have to listen to the music constantly playing.

"I love the LOR system, as my erratic work shifts keep me away many nights, and with LOR start and stop times are completely automatic.

"One of the songs I have sequenced is 'Deck The Halls' by the modern country group trio SHeDAISY (from Utah). I have justalways loved it.

Anyway, one night there was a knock at the door and when I opened it, there was a man and woman standing there. They said they liked the display and were amazed at the show. Then he said that we had used 'her' song. It took me a minute to realize I was standing face to face with one of the sisters from SHeDAISY, Kelsi Osborn!

"When people love and appreciate what I've done… well, that's it for me!

"Every year I have to out-do the previous year's display. I'm also working towards manufacturing and selling several items in my display."

Dave Horting
West Haven, Utah, USA

The synchronization of music and lights is the key factor for Dave Horting in making his display in Utah, USA.

An 144-channel computer system mean the lights come on even when Dave's at work!

Music is played through a special transmitter direct to car radios, so the neighbours aren't disturbed.

Norwich night lights

"AT ONE TIME, MY GIRLFRIEND WAS GOING TO EMBARK ON A PROJECT CONTRASTING CHRISTMAS LIGHTS WITH THE NEON OF SHINJUKU IN TOKYO. HOWEVER, SHE DECIDED AGAINST IT."

"There are loads of houses in Norwich which decorate their houses which is fantastic. Each year our local newspaper, the *Norwich Evening News*, and the city council run a competition offering a prize to the best-lit home. This house was nominated in 2003 – it may even have won, actually.

"I took the image because myself and my girlfriend, Sarah, just love Christmas lights. Sarah is the Course Leader of the Fine Art course at Norwich School of Art and Design and I am the Marketing Manager there. Sarah had an exhibition in Tokyo, and at one time was going to embark on a project contrasting Christmas lights with the advertising neon of Shinjuku in Tokyo, Japan. However, she decided against it."

David Girling
Sprowston, Norwich, England

oh brother!

"WHEN MY BROTHER BOUGHT OUR PREVIOUS HOUSE, WE GAVE HIM A FEW OF OUR OLD DECORATIONS. WE CREATED A MONSTER."

"My husband Marc has been going at it for around 25 years and each Christmas we add a bit more. One year we decided not to decorate, but when the limos started to come by we realized that we couldn't take the year off! We had to put the display up in record time so we didn't disappoint the onlookers. We won't make that mistake again.

"Storage during the year isn't a problem. When we built the house, we had a special opening put in the garage attic to allow for huge items to get through easily.

"My brother bought our previous house and we gave him a few of our old decorations. We created a monster. He even beat us in a 'Griswald' lighting contest in 2004. No more ideas from us to him!

"Our old house was an icon because we lived there for 15 years, and thousands of people came by each season to see our display. We lost our onlookers to my brother so we're trying to regain the masses."

Marc & Deb Hansen
LaVista, Nebraska USA

Llori loves lights!

"I ALSO DECORATE MY JACKETS AND HATS WITH LIGHTS TO ACCESSORIZE WITH MY BALCONY. IT GETS THE NEIGHBORS TALKING."

"I'm in an apartment with a balcony, so my display isn't very big, but I can accomplish much brightness and computerized synchronicity.

"I do it to show off and provoke more tenants in my building to decorate – I'd like to imagine that one day the whole apartment block will be sprayed with lights. Over-decorated balconies are funny.

"I love lights – they seem to bring out the best in people. I also decorate my jackets and hats with LED lights to accessorize with my balcony. It gets the neighbors talking."

"What do my family and friends think about it? They try not to – they think I'm mental! Only my husband enjoys it... to a point!"

Llori Stein
Falls Church, Virginia, USA

Christmas
with the Koretzes

"WE HAVE A SHIP'S CARGO CONTAINER AT THE BACK OF OUR PROPERTY. IT'S 40 FEET LONG AND EIGHT FEET WIDE AND IT'S FULL OF DECORATIONS."

"We have always decorated, but only to this extreme since we moved to this house in 1998. It all started that July, when my wife, Kim, and I were doing a walk through with the electrician during construction. The electrician asked us if he wanted some outlets under the roof edge.

'Why? You can't reach them,' I said.

'For Christmas lights...'

'Yes, we need them, and, yes, he will put up some lights,' replied Kim.

I just looked at Kim and said, 'Honey, you don't know what you're starting.'

"Our display has become so large, we are working on it all year long, whether it's looking for new things to add or pre-ordering new inflatables.

"We have a ship's cargo container at the back of our property. It's 40 feet long and eight feet wide and it's full of decorations. We start getting the display out of the container during the second week of October, and the lights start going up about a week or two later. It takes about 240 hours to set it up and about a month to take it all down and pack it up.

"All the family help – myself, my wife and our three son's (Zack aged 10, JL, 4, and Lance 3). The future of the display will be in JL and Lance's hands – they love Christmas."

Butch Koretz and family
Yuma, Arizona, USA

The Koretz family's display has grown from 5,000 lights in 1998 to over 70,000.

An average of 2,000 people per night (4,000 on weekends) came to see the 2004 display.

A giant computerised tree was introduced in 2003.

Even the seats are illuminated!

The Koretz family and Santa.

Lightasmic!®

"EVERYTHING FROM THE ROOF TO THE SIDES OF THE HOUSE TO THE YARD AND DRIVEWAY WAS COVERED IN LIGHTS."

"I started off in 1991, aged nine, with just a few strands of lights on the bushes at my nana's home. Seeing how happy that made her, I was determined to outdo myself the following year.

"Over the years, I began using many more lights and constructing other elements and wooden characters and adding special effects. By 1998 my holiday displays began receiving media attention.

"I did the final display at my own home in 2001. Known as 'Lightasmic!', it used 185,000 computer-controlled lights to produce a 10-minute show synchronized to holiday music. Everything from the roof to the end of the driveway was covered in lights.

"I then turned Lightasmic!® into a company and moved my light show to the parking lot of Stier's RV. That show included 500,000 lights and snow machines to provide a 'snow zone' in the California desert. The show was featured on 'America's Greatest Christmas Decorations' on NBC in 2002. From there, I was invited by members of the California Living Museum (CALM) Foundation Board to have Lightasmic!® hosted at CALM and that display was built on a foundation of two million lights."

Josh Barnett
Bakersfield, California, USA

Josh started out putting up a few strands of lights for his nana in 1991. By 2002, his displays had got a little bit bigger!

Josh Barnett's incredible display at the California Living Museum (CALM) was built on the foundation of two million lights.

Planet Christmas: Josh's display at the California Living Museum also featured Santa and his reindeer circling a 20-foot diameter animated globe.

Bill & Peg's
christmas venture

"THE 'CHRISTMAS ROOM' IS LEFT UP THROUGHOUT THE YEAR AND WE OFTEN ENJOY A SPECIAL QUIET MEAL IN IT."

"The tradition of Lobethal's Christmas Lights began nearly 60 years ago when a few businessmen hand-painted globes to decorate their Main Street shops for the Christmas season. This tradition spread and today over 80 per cent of all homes and businesses in the village 'light up' for Christmas with a variety of spectacular displays.

"When we moved to Lobethal in December 1983 we followed the town's tradition by having a few lights. Each year Peg and I said that we really should do a bit more, but it was not until 1986 that we finally made the effort. Since then, we've added to our display each year and it now consists of around 35,000 lights and 100 wooden cut-outs (many of which we have made ourselves).

"For Christmas 1998 we added a 'Christmas Room' (pictured) which is left up throughout the year, and we often enjoy a special quiet meal in it. The room is not open to the public, but can be viewed through large windows.

"We usually get between 3,000 and 3,500 entries in our Visitors' Book (but we estimate that only between five and ten percent sign), and visitors have come from as many as 35 different countries."

Bill & Peg Chartres
Lobethal, South Australia

The power of two

"WE WOULD GO BIGGER, BUT WE DO NOT HAVE ENOUGH AVAILABLE POWER, SO WE'VE BEEN AT 100,000 LIGHTS OR SO FOR THE PAST THREE YEARS…"

"Our display is a traditional theme Christmas with something for all ages. It attracts 50,000 visitors per season and at times, we have as many as 500 people walking around our property.

"There is a local group of decorators here in Central Florida. I wish we could go and see their displays, but once we light up we've got to be here. I have to direct traffic many nights for two to four hours.

"I think our favorite feature is the way we decorate our garage with antique furniture including a 1949 fireplace. It reminds us of our childhood Christmases in the '50s.

"Electric costs around US$630 for two houses for 20 days and five hours each night. We tap the neighbors' power for 80 amps in addition to our 200-amp service from which 165 amps are being drawn continuously. We would go bigger, but we do not have enough available power, so we've been at 100,000 lights or so for the past three years.

"My wife, Betty, was my main inspiration for getting me started doing this (her family all decorate lavishly). Sadly, she has breast cancer and is now undergoing chemotherapy (April 2005). I am hoping we will be able to continue the display together for many more years."

Rob and Betty Petersen
Winter Park, Florida, USA

The bright lights of Berkshire

"This man from Woodley, Berkshire in England decorated his house to raise money for the Daisy's Dream charity which supports bereaved children and families."

"Santa got himself a jet to help him deliver presents and the Buscot Babies Special Care Unit at the Royal Berkshire hospital received money collected from passers-by."

37 years and counting...

"THE TALL GREEN AND BLUE TREES HAVE OVER 1,000 ROPE LIGHTS – LARRY SPENT TWO DAYS IN THESE TREES WITH A CHERRY PICKER."

"We started very small in Hollywood, Florida, in 1966. After 19 years, we moved to Kissimmee, also in Florida, and this is our 2003 display.

"The tall green and blue trees have over 1,000 rope lights – Larry spent two days in these trees with a cherry picker putting up all the lights. Our blue tree has 600 rope lights (150 of each color) and the tree lights up one color at a time, and then all four colors light up.

"We have now moved to Pilot Mountain in North Carolina where we will continue the tradition starting in 2005. God bless America and our home with the moon watching over us."

Larry & Rachel Charpiat
Kissimmee, Florida, USA

Moose
on the
roof!

"**I**nstallation time for this display in 2003 was 63 hours. The trickiest thing was hoisting two animated moose onto the roof and chimney. My wife helps from the ground while I lift them by cable to the roof.

"Several houses nearby compete with us and on Christmas Eve all homes put out luminaries with candles at dusk. It is a tradition for people from all over town to drive through the neighborhood, and drop off donations to the local food bank on their way.

"How does my electricity bill compare to normal at Christmas time? Erm, my wife does not have access to this information, and I prefer not to answer so that I can continue my display each year!"

Ricky Thames
Midland, Texas, USA

cornish snowscape

"MY FAVOURITE DECORATIVE FEATURE IS THE ARTIFICIAL SNOW ON THE FRONT LAWN BECAUSE WE DON'T GET MUCH SNOW IN THIS PART OF CORNWALL."

"We have over 12,000 bulbs, almost 100 metres of rope light 90 blow molds, 80 wire frames some of which are animated with motors. There's also a Father Christmas in front of a glowing fire on the roof of the garage complete with a Christmas tree and stars to light up the sky. My favourite decorative feature is the artificial snow on the front lawn, though, because we don't get much snow in this part of Cornwall. It really stands out during the day and I've had many nice comments from people about it.

"I start work at the beginning of October to assemble everything in time to light up during the last week in November. My wife Carol helps when she can, mostly telling me where to put everything! The hardest thing to put up are always the roof lights – they need to go up before the weather changes. I don't go up on that roof unless it's dry.

"We have been decorating since 1998 and have collected for a children's hospice charity for the last three years. The money we raise helps children with terminal illnesses and the families of those children."

Glenwood J. Collings
Par, Cornwall, England

Kicki and Knut!

"THE LIGHTS ARE ON FROM 1 DECEMBER UNTIL THE SECOND WEEK IN JANUARY ON THE DAY OF 'KNUT', WHICH IS AN OLD TRADITION IN SWEDEN."

"Hi! We've got more decorations than ever – it's growing out of our hands!

"Several newspapers and television crews have been here and hundreds of people walk by each evening. We turn on the lights on the 1 December and they are on between 3pm and 10pm until the second week in January on the day of 'Knut', which is an old tradition in Sweden.

"Many people have found us via the PlanetChristmas website and come to look and take some pictures. Many regards to the people of Sweden, the US of A and the whole world. Christmas hugs!"

Kicki Brunzell
Sweden

Super street lights

"Happy kids play near a giant Christmas bauble in Seoul, South Korea, where Christmas is one of the biggest holidays."

"Santa jumps from roof to roof in this natty aerial display in Funchal, Madeira."

"Some 410,000 festive lights illuminate the zelkova trees on a street in Omotesando, Tokyo, Japan."

Nutcrackin' Christmas!

"**W**e have seven inflatables, 20,000 lights, 28 wireframes (mostly homemade), two giant Nutcrackers guard the garage, and about 40 blowmolds are spread around. A giant inflatable Santa waves from atop our rear deck to the street behind us.

"A large LED sign instructs drivers to tune their radio to 92.9FM to hear Christmas music and a special message from us. And on the Friday before Christmas, Santa visits and we have hot chocolate and cookies for the kids.

"We just love decorating. Unfortunately, no-one else in our area goes so extreme in their Christmas decoration, but we have inspired some to begin decorating."

Marshall and Laurie Rice
Troy, Illinois, USA

Born to do it

"MY MOTHER SAID ONE OF MY VERY FIRST WORDS WAS 'IGHTS' WITHOUT THE 'L'."

"When I was setting up my website (welovechristmaslights.com) and trying to answer why I did all this, I wrote that we never had lights outside when I was growing up and that the lack of lights at my own house probably triggered an instinct to go crazy with lights as an adult. My mother quickly corrected me. I was born in November so by my second Christmas I was pretty aware of my surroundings. She said one of my very first words was 'ights' without the 'l'. Later on, when I could count, I would count the number of houses where I saw lights when we were driving around in the car. When I was old enough to drive, I would drive my friends around to find the best light displays. So I guess I have really been obsessed with Christmas lights most of my life.

"Because we are a military family (Air Force), we move about every three years and we end up meeting a lot of people because of our displays. And the people that I have met through PlanetChristmas from all over the world are some of my best friends in the world. One of the highlights of my year is when some of us can get together and see each other face to face."

Jeff Womack
Schertz, Texas, USA

Santa's house

"**D**anny Meikle transformed his home into a dazzling festive wonderland of one million christmas lights. He won £10,000 from break-fast television show GMTV for the best Christmas decorations in the UK, and donated at least half of the money to charity."

Not too bright for you?

"John Dacosta's house in Mississauga, Ontario, Canada, has over 60,000 bulbs and visitors are asked to leave a donation for charity."

Santa hangs tough!

"A couple look on as Santa holds on to the roof of this home in Hamburg, Germany."

Tribute to mom

"AFTER A FEW YEARS OF NO LIGHTS OR CHRISTMAS, I SLOWLY STARTED PUTTING UP A LITTLE BIT EACH YEAR. IT'S KINDA LIKE LETTING MOM KNOW WE HAVEN'T FORGOTTEN HER."

"I'm 24 years old and have been decorating the house with lots of lights for about six or seven years myself, but as a kid my dad used to do it during the mid-80s at my grandmother's house close by. He was featured in newspapers and my sisters and me were on the news as kids on Christmas Day for his display almost 20 years ago.

"Then, on 19 December 1987, my mom passed away and Christmas stopped for a few years around here. It hurt us all a lot. But after a few years of no lights or Christmas, I slowly started putting up a little bit each year. It's kinda like letting mom know we haven't forgotten her.

"It's now getting bigger and bigger – in 2004, there was around 105,000 lights and 16 channels of animated lighting control. I can't wait for the next Christmas season to come."

Brett Morrow
Hatboro, Pennsylvania, USA

Brett Morrow's talent for Christmas lighting is inherited from his father.

Tree-mendous!

"It took a brave person to volunteer to put up these lights in Phoenix, Arizona, USA!"

"A tropical twist to the Christmas theme in Springfield, Massachussets, USA."

Germanic delights!

"**T**he owner of this house in Obermeitlingen in Germany has been decorating his home and garden with thousands of lights on the inside and outside every year, and his house has become a major attraction for visitors to the Bavarian village during the Christmas season."

Toy Story

"Our display consists of 45,000 lights, several large inflatables and blow-mold characters, a Santa's Workshop and our Polar Bear Café.

  "We are an official collection spot for the Marine Corps' 'Toys for Tots' campaign and last year we collected hundreds of new toys that were given out to local needy children.

  "We even get a lot of daytime visitors – not sure why, but we do..."

Greg Parcell
Geneva, Illinois, US

White wedding vow

"It wasn't until I got married that I was hooked by an after-Christmas sale. I bought several hundred dollars worth of lights, but only clear bulbs. That was something that was in our 'wedding vows' – no colored lights!

  "It was about 16 years ago when I did my first display. Now, I do it for my children. I want my kids to remember that Dad did this for them at Christmas."

Robert Burton
Fayetteville, Georgia, USA

Bad dog, Clifford!

"It takes about one week to put up our whole display. My son-in-law helps with the icicle lights because I'm unable to get on the roof due to age and metal knees!

"My favourite part is the Elves toys factory. The elf on a ladder comes on, and then pushes the stuff down the funnel, and a puff of smoke comes out of the first chimney. The letters of 'TOYS' all come on individually and then the left-hand gear wheel comes on as well. The two letter 'O' gear wheels turn and mesh together. The arrow on the dial has three positions – at its highest, a parcel pops out of the right-hand chimney and then is seen in mid-air, before the elf in sleigh catches it and lowers it onto the other parcels in the sleigh.

"There are carpenter elves who hammer and saw, plus we have had an elf on a scooter, an elf on a skateboard and Edith the elf juggling balls.

"In another area, 'Clifford' the dog just happens to animatedly lift his leg (and tail) and pee on the North Pole! Up on the wall, Santa, on his motorbike drags all the reindeer in three trailers. Rudolph brings up the rear because of his shiny red nose!"

Don & Jacquie McNab
Whakatane, New Zealand

Christmas banquet

"Feast your eyes on this scrumptious lights display in London, England!"

Lit up like a Christmas tree!

"Some Londoners just buy a Christmas tree, some go that extra mile..."

Going Dutch

"These pictures taken in Helmond in 2003 show a growing trend for extreme decoration of houses in the Netherlands."

Why? Because it's Christmas...

"THIS CAR-STOPPER HAS A SEVEN-SPEAKER, SURROUND-SOUND, HOME THEATER SYSTEM PUMPING OUT THE SOUNDS OF THE MARK BUZA ORCHESTRA."

"With over 20,000 lights, this car-stopper has a seven-speaker, surround-sound, home-theater system pumping out the sounds of The Mark Buza Orchestra and their CD, 'Because It's Christmas.' If it's too cold outside, the onlookers can turn on their car stereos to 95.5FM and listen to it in the comfort of their vehicle.

"It's all about attention to detail. We love to take the commercial and store-bought lights and customize them. Those reindeer on the deck (see page 119) really do fly up and down thanks to a home-made motorized system. Santa Claus always makes a stop on Christmas Eve, gives out candy canes and listens to last-minute gift requests.

"This is our gift to the community. May you have a blessed Christmas and we'll see you next year."

The Buza family
Binghampton, New York

The Buza family's display in New York is all about attention to detail.

Santa rides his train through the snowman village.

Now that's what you call a garage!

Stars & Stripes

"These American families wear their national colours with pride..."

Even politicians get festive!

"A policeman keeps an eye on the British Prime Minister's home at Number 10 Downing Street (and the PM's Christmas tree)."

"A lavishly decorated tree brings a festive flavour to the Capitol Building in Washington, USA."

Nugget City delight

"WE EXPANDED INTO THE BACKYARD BECAUSE WE RAN OUT OF ROOM."

"Hi to all you Christmas enthusiasts! My name is Don Hill and my wife, Chris, and I have been decorating for over a decade. Each year the display gets bigger and bigger, so much so that in 2004 we expanded into the backyard because we ran out of room.

"We have several themes going on, separated by candy cane lanes. There's the Santa scene (I dress up as Santa on the weekends – the kids love it), a scene with a four-carriage playground-size train and church with a steeple and the Nativity featured in the center of the front yard. The Nativity scene is our favourite because that is what Christmas is really about.

"In the back yard, we have a replica of a Colorado mining town (Nugget City) all lit up with decorated Christmas trees and buck board and other animated characters. We use everything from rope lights and inflatables to wooden hand-painted figures, and the lights on the house are controlled by music.

"Our house is now on the Denver lights tour so people come by and we encourage them to get out and look around. Indeed, in 2004, we actually won the Denver lights display award. Kinda exciting, huh?"

Don & Chris Hill
Denver, Colorado, USA

Don and Chris Hill's amazing display includes a four-carriage, playground-size train.

Unsurprisingly, the Hills' award-winning Christmas display is a must-see on the Denver lights tour.

The Nativity scene is the centrepiece of Don and Chris Hill's frontyard because "that is what Christmas is really about."

Keith's happy accident

"I ALWAYS BUY MORE DECORATIONS THAN MY WIFE THINKS I SHOULD DURING THE AFTER-CHRISTMAS SALES…"

"Why do I do it? For the religious aspects. To remind people in a simple way what the meaning of Christmas is and always will be – that it is the time to welcome Christ, not man. I also decorate because it's a fun, family hobby for all to participate in.

"I always buy more decorations than my wife thinks I should during the after-Christmas sales. One year, unbeknown to her, I had bought a couple of thousand lights and had them in my car trunk. We were both driving around a corner one after the other, and my wife accidentally rear-ended my car with hers. My trunk popped open and the light boxes fell out onto the street. I couldn't tell if she was madder about the lights or the fact that she accidentally hit me! We laugh about it now…"

Keith Portell
Jacksonville, Florida, USA

Brazil-liant!

"A house in Curitaba, Brazil, spangled with hundreds of white lights and Christmas decorations."

Norm's obsession

"MANY PEOPLE THINK THAT WE ARE 'NUTSO', BUT MOST APPRECIATE THE EFFORT WE'VE MADE AND OUR EXPRESSION OF THE CHRISTMAS SPIRIT."

"I have been doing holiday lighting for about 30 years now, and every year seems to be a bit more extravagant. Our outdoor display takes about three months to complete and completely surrounds our house. I stopped counting lights and now think in terms of watts and amps. This past year we used 38 dedicated 20 amp circuits and pulled 550 amps/60,000 watts of power. Our Christmas electric bill is about six-and-a-half times more that our normal bill, averaging about $1,200 to $1,300 for a three-week period.

"It started out as a hobby but has turned into a obsession. The enjoyment I give other people seems to drive me. It's a lot of work, to say the least. Many people think that we are 'nutso', but most appreciate the effort we've made and our expression of the Christmas spirit.

"The inside of our house is all decked out as well. Last Christmas we had 25 decorated trees indoors, each with a different theme. The indoor stuff pulls about an additional 100 amps of power.

"During the year, we store all of the decorations in our 2,200 square-foot basement. Just about the entire area is all Christmas!"

Norm Flowers
Rochester, Michigan, USA

Pole apart!

"This is the third Christmas that I've decorated my house. I use 60 metres of rope light on the house and 20 metres of light on the trees. Putting everything up takes about ten hours – I do everything alone.

"I do it because I saw a film with decorated houses. I do it for fun and because nobody else in my city does it. In the first year, my family and friends said that I couldn't do it, but when I finished they said it was super.

"Now I have done it, my friend says he will do this too next year. The year after that, another friend will do this as well. I hope to see a lot more decorated houses in Jaworzno... but it's good to be the first!"

Jakub Czopik
Jaworzno, Poland

Recyclable Rudolph!

"AFTER THE HOLIDAYS, 'RUDOLPH' BECOMES GARDEN MULCH FOR ACID-LOVING PLANTS."

"It was 1996, the first Christmas after my mother and brother died and I needed 'light therapy' so I bought strands of lights to wrap around our large oak tree.

"One night I sat on the front stoop and noticed the lighted limbs looked like antlers. The next day, I started raking pine straw from neighbors' yards and collected discarded lumber from local construction sites. Neighbors, who were sceptical about the project during its rather shabby early phase, eventually rallied around offering sleigh bells, ribbons and glass bulbs for eyes. Within a week the creature, about eight-feet tall and 30 feet long, was built.

"It is now a neighborhood tradition and adults and children bring little wagonloads of pine straw they've raked from their yards to help build 'Rudolph'. Construction begins on Thanksgiving Day and, with the neighbors' help, it's finished in three days and ceremoniously lit on the following Sunday.

"The creature makes the local TV and newspapers and draws large crowds every year. He's also 100 per cent recyclable, so after the holidays, 'Rudolph' becomes garden mulch for acid-loving plants!"

Kathy Hall
Houston, Texas, USA

Love the lights?

**Do you wanna see some more of the best displays from around the world?
Check out these web links...**

...And then there were Christmas Lights
www.floridachristmasdisplay.com

Animated Lighting™
www.animatedlighting.com/showcase

Brad's Christmas world
www.bradschristmasworld.tripod.com

Bill & Peg's Christmas Down Under
users.chariot.net.au/~chartres

Christmas At Pebble Creek Drive
www.pebblecreeklights.com

Christmas creations from Australia
www.geocities.com/SiliconValley/Screen/9808

Christmas House
www.christmashouse.0catch.com/index.html

ChristmasUtah
www.christmasutah.com

Christmas Wonders
www.christmaswonders.homestead.com/2004_Pictures.html

Colorado Christmas
www.coloradoxmas.com

Computer Christmas Lights
www.computerchristmaslights.com

Digital Christmas
home.earthlink.net/~jfaszl1882/indexnew.htm

Gary's Christmas Wonderland
cscs_2.tripod.com/xmas/home.htm

Holidastic!
www.holidastic.net.tc

Hudson Christmas
www.hudsonchristmas.com

**Kindla crafts - Electric train and
Christmas Display**
www.angelfire.com/tx5/brycekindla

King of the Holiday Inflatables
www.kingofholidayinflatables.com

Koretz family
www.koretz.neptune.com

Larry & Rachel Charpiat's Christmas Extravaganza
home.earthlink.net/~xmasdisplay

Lightasmic!®
www.lightasmic.com

Lighting Spectacular
www.intuitiveideas.com

Lightup.ca
www.lightup.ca/main.htm

Maddog 'n' Miracles Christmas
www.io.com/~maddog/photos_x.htm

Magic Christmas
www.magicchristmas.org

Nature comes to light
www.richmondkinsmen.com/christmas/index.htm

Norton's Winter Wonderland
www.nortonswinterwonderland.com

Pensacola Lights
www.pensacolalights.com

PlanetChristmas
www.planetchristmas.com

Portell's Christmas Web Site
www.keithportell.net

The Sharp's House Of Lights
members.aol.com/elloco7/index.html

Rob and Betty Petersen
home.earthlink.net/~rob35

Sylvan Lights
users.rttinc.com/~sylvanlights

TwasTheNightBefore
www.twasthenightbefore.com

If you would like to add your website link to the
PlanetChristmas website and our list for future
editions of this book, please email details to
Chuck Smith at csmith@planetchristmas.com

Picture Credits

A big thank you to all the PlanetChristmas contributors and Christmas lights enthusiasts who gave permission to use their personal photographs in this book.

List of agency images:

Page(s)

20/21	Norm Betts/Rex Features (Canadian Pacific Transport train, Canada)
22	Nourse/Accent Alaska Steven/Photolibrary (Seward, Alaska, USA)
23	Rick Sounders/Photolibrary (taken in a field... somewhere!)
26	Clineff Kindra/Index Stock Imagery/Photolibrary (Springfield, Massachusetts, USA)
27	Richard Austin/Rex Features (Lyme Regis, Dorset, England)
32	David Gray/Reuters (Martin Place, Sydney, Australia)
33	Mauricio Lima/Getty Images (Sao Paulo, Brazil)
40/41	Action Press/Rex Features (Bremen Habenhausen, Germany)
46	Tony Kyraicou/Rex Features (The London Eye, London, England)
47	Tony Kyraicou/Rex Features (The London Eye, London, England)
54	Owen Humphreys/PA/Empics (Cowgate, Newcastle, England)
80	David Hartley/Rex Features (Woodley, Berkshire, England)
81	David Hartley/Rex Features (Bradfield, Berkshire, England)
90	Chung Sung-Jun/Stringer/Getty Images (Seoul, South Korea)
91	Butcher Rex/John Arnold Images/Photolibrary (Funchal, Madeira, Portugal)
92/93	Kazuhiro Nogi/Getty Images (Omotesando, Tokyo, Japan)
98	Andrew Milligan/PA/Empics (England)
99	Andrew Milligan/PA/Empics (England)
100	CP Canadian Press/Canada Press/Empics (Ontario, Canada)
101	DPA Deutsche-Press-Agentur/DPA/Empics (Hamburg, Germany)
106	Ewing Galloway/Index Stock Imagery/Photolibrary (Phoenix, Arizona, USA)
107	Clineff Kindra/Image Stock Imagery/Photolibrary (Springfield, Massachussets, USA)
108/09	DPA Deutsche-Press-Agentur/ DPA/Empics (Obermeitlingen, Germany)
112	Ilpo Musto/Rex Features (London, England)
113	Per Lindgren/Rex Features (London, England)
114a&b	Alegmeen Nederlands persuburau/ANP/Empics (Helmond, Netherlands)
115	Alegmeen Nederlands Persuburau/ANP/Empics (Helmond, Netherlands)
120	David McNew/Getty Images (Mission Viejo, California, USA)
121	David McNew/Getty Images (Orange County, California, USA)
122	Alisdair Macdonald/Rex Features (London, England)
123	John Hartman/Rex Features (Washington, USA)
134/35	Orlando Kissner/Stringer/AFP/Getty Images, (Curitiba, Brazil)

Wannabe top of the tree?

Enter the PlanetChristmas Worldwide Outdoor Christmas Lighting Contest!

In 2004, PlanetChristmas launched the first-ever global outdoor lighting contest. There was US$1,000 in cash and decoration coupons on offer as prizes, but more importantly, the chance to be honoured as the world's greatest!

Hundreds of entries flooded in from around the globe, the quality of light displays was exceptional and the judges agonized over their choices. Judging was based on originality, Christmas spirit, contribution to the community and testimonials.

The 'Standard Display' prize (for houses with under 50,000 lights) was shared between Martin and Andrew Lindsay (Ontario, Canada) with their amazing computerized light show, and Ron Lister (Kissimmee, Florida, USA) whose computerized light show, hand-crafted elements and special song dedicated to troops stationed overseas won the plaudits.

Rich Faucher, in New Castle, Delaware, USA, prevailed in the 'Over-The-Top' category (for houses with more lights and special effects than you can count). His commitment to the community, 500,000 lights as well as collecting 'Toys for Tots' and the Ronald McDonald house impressed the judges as a shining example of the Christmas spirit.

Inspired? Well, the competition is open to all-comers, so get decorating. For further details of how to enter this year's competition, just log on to planetchristmas.com.